Two Facts & a Fib
Zoo Animals

This Book Belongs To

_____

To Sydney & Hudson who love the zoo
and Venci who is not allowed in

TIGER

Fact or Fib?

1. Tigers can eat 100 pounds of food or 400 hamburgers in one night.

2. Tigers hate the water because they are not good swimmers.

3. There are more tigers living privately as pets than there are in the wild.

Meerkat

Fact or Fib?

1. Meerkats stop growing after two years.

2. A meerkat's belly acts like a solar panel that absorbs heat and keeps them warm.

3. Meerkats have ears that can open and close in order for them to keep sand out when they are digging.

Zebra

Fact or Fib?

1. Zebras have large muscular bodies, long legs and one toe on each foot.

2. Baby zebras are born with their black and white stripes.

3. Zebras stand up while sleeping.

Prairie Dog

Fact or Fib?

1. Two prairie dogs recognize each other by touching their front teeth together.

2. Prairie dogs do not drink water and eat only plants.

3. Most prairie dogs can see the second they are born.

Anteater

Fact or Fib?

1. A baby anteater rides on its mother's back for about six months.

2. Anteaters do not have teeth. Instead, they use their long, sticky tongues to pick up ants and other insects.

3. The anteater has trouble sleeping and only sleeps 2 hours a night.

Lion

Fact or Fib?

1. A group of lions is called a pride.

2. A male lion's mane protects him when he fights.

3. Lions can run up to 70 miles per hour.

Monkey

Fact or Fib?

1. Monkeys have an IQ of 174.

2. Monkeys are common household pets.

3. Monkeys have been known to eat dirt and soil when they do not find food.

WARTHOG

Fact or Fib?

1. A warthog's tail swings side to side when they run.

2. Warthogs have developed thick knee pads on their front knees since they have to kneel down to eat.

3. Baby warthogs run in a straight line behind their mother.

Camel

Fact or Fib?

1. Camels can go for two months without water and can run for hours without stopping.

2. Camels store water in their humps.

3. A camel's stomach is made up of 3 compartments.

Kangaroo

Fact or Fib?

1. Oddly enough kangaroos can not walk backwards.

2. Kangaroos have very powerful legs and can sometimes jump three times their own height.

3. Kangaroos are scared of water and can't swim.

Polar Bear

Fact or Fib?

1. A polar bear's fur is pure white.

2. Female polar bears usually only weigh about half as much as males.

3. Polar bears can swim at a rate of 6 miles per hour in sea water at sub-zero temperatures.

Giraffe

Fact or Fib?

1. A giraffe's heart is the smallest of all zoo animals.

2. Giraffes have very long tongues and can lick their own ears.

3. When giraffes walk they move both right legs forward, then both left.

Cheetah

Fact or Fib?

1. Cheetahs can reach 60 mph in 3 seconds. They are the fastest creatures on earth.

2. All cheetahs travel together in groups.

3. Cheetahs have long black lines that run from their eyes to their mouth called tears.

RHINOCEROS

Fact or Fib?

1. A rhinoceros has a large brain that is relative to its large body size.

2. A rhinoceros gets mud on its back to protect its skin from getting sunburn.

3. A rhinoceros is not really bad tempered. They often charge because they are startled.

Did you find the fib?

ANSWERS

Tiger: #2
Tigers love the water and are very good swimmers.

Meerkat: #1
Meerkats become fully grown within six months of their birth.

Zebra: #2
Baby zebras are born with brown and white stripes. As they get older, the stripes turn black and white.

Prairie Dog: #3
All prairie dogs are blind and furless at birth.

Anteater: #3
Anteaters hunt for food at night and sleep as much as 15 hours a day.

Lion: #3
Lions can only run up to 50 miles per hour, but can jump as far as 36 feet.

Monkey: #2
There are only about 15,000 monkeys that are kept as pets in the United States.